The Truth About Love:

Quotations & Reflections

The Truth About Love:

Quotations & Reflections

Edited by Alison Bing

BARNES
&NOBLE
BOOKS
NEW YORK

The quotes in this book have been drawn from many sources, and are assumed to be accurate as quoted in their previously published forms. Although every effort has been made to verify the quotes and sources, the publisher cannot guarantee their perfect accuracy.

2003 Barnes & Noble Books

ISBN 0-7607-4067-4

Printed and bound in the United States of America

M 9 8 7 6 5 4 3 2 1

GREETINGS ALL YOU FLEDGLING DON JUANS AND Donna Juanas,

Ever wish you could become an expert on love without having to pay for your Ph.D. from the School of Hard Knocks? Well, your wish is my command (though as a love expert, you should know better than to get used to that kind of thing).

This is the truth about love as only our great poets, wits, and bon vivants can tell it: wisdom that is painless, odorless and easily absorbed, without all the greasy residue of lesser brands. This topical treatment contains potent words of desire, inspiration, and perspiration to serve as an aphrodisiac for promising moments—and a salve for awkward ones. Apply them to your own condition judiciously.

Here's hoping your love comes in the many-splendored variety pack, or at least economy-sized...

Sincerely,

Alison Bing

who would like to issue an APB for her thunder, which was stolen by Marlene Deitrich when she said: "I love quotations because it is a joy to find thoughts one might have, beautifully expressed with much authority by someone recognized wiser than oneself."

Falling In It

O tell me the truth about love…
Can it pull extraordinary faces?
Is it usually sick on a swing?
Does it spend all its time at the races,
Or fiddling with pieces of string?

    —W. H. AUDEN, "O Tell Me the Truth About Love"

Everyone admits that love is wonderful and necessary, yet no one can agree on what it is.

    —DIANE ACKERMAN, *A Natural History of Love*

What is this thing called love? What? Is this thing called love? What is this thing called? Love.

—COLE PORTER, "What Is This Thing Called Love?"

Holy forgiveness! mercy! charity! faith! Holy!
　　Ours! bodies! suffering! magnanimity!
Holy the supernatural extra brilliant intelligent
　　kindness of the soul!

—ALLEN GINSBERG, footnote to *Howl*

Love is the extremely difficult realization that something other than oneself is real.

—IRIS MURDOCH, "The Sublime and the Good"

Gravitation is not responsible for people falling in love.

—attributed to ALBERT EINSTEIN

Your love threw me down
in a land of wonder
it ambushed me like the scent
of a woman stepping into an elevator…
It surprised me
as I sat on my suitcase
waiting for the train of days
I forgot the days
I traveled with you
to the land of wonder.

—Nizar Qabbani, "Poems"

No one on this planet ever really chooses each other. I mean, it's all a question of quantum physics, molecular attraction and timing.

—Ron Shelton, *Bull Durham*

Whoso loves
Believes the impossible.

—ELIZABETH BARRETT BROWNING, *Aurora Leigh*

Love is … the open sesame to every soul.

—ELIZABETH CADY STANTON, in a speech, 1860

This is our
creation,
it's growing
this very
instant, kicking up
sand or eating
out of our hand.
Catch it,
don't let it slip away!

—PABLO NERUDA, "Ode to the Present Moment"

At First Sight

I see you and my heart has found
A reason for mankind and an apology.
How slight a chance brings on our destiny!

—Lucy Boston, "Farewell to a Trappist"

I never saw so sweet a face
As that I stood before.
My heart has lost its dwelling-place
And can return no more.

—John Clare, "First Love"

The power of a glance has been so much abused in love stories, that is has come to be disbelieved in. Few people dare now say that two beings have fallen in love because they have looked at each other. Yet it is in this way that love begins… Nothing is more real than these great shocks which two souls give each other in exchanging this spark.

—Victor Hugo, *Les Misérables*

Beauty is not in the face;
Beauty is a light in the heart.

—Kahlil Gibran, "The Sayings of the Brook"

Many a man has fallen in love with a girl in a light so dim he would not have chosen a suit by it.

—Maurice Chevalier,
as quoted in *News Summaries*, 1955

I was about half in love with her by the time we sat down. That's the thing about girls. Every time they do something pretty, even if they're not much to look at, or even if they're sort of stupid, you fall half in love with them, and then you never know where the hell you are.

—J. D. SALINGER, *Catcher in the Rye*

Let the world know you as you are, not as you think you should be, because sooner or later, if you are posing, you will forget the pose, and then where are you?

—FANNY BRICE, as quoted in
The Fabulous Fanny, by Norman Katkov

If thou must love me, let it be for naught
Except for love's sake only. Do not say
"I love her for her smile...her look...her way
Of speaking gently...for a trick of thought
That falls in well with mine, and certes brought
A sense of pleasant ease on such a day..."
But love me for love's sake, that evermore
Thou may'st love on, through love's eternity.

—ELIZABETH BARRETT BROWNING,
"If Thou Must Love Me," *Sonnets from the Portuguese*

The perception of beauty is a moral test.

—HENRY DAVID THOREAU, *Journal 5*

Beauty is in the eye of the beholder.

—MARGARET WOLFE HUNGERFORD,
a.k.a. "The Duchess," *Molly Bawn*

Be my mistress short or tall
And distorted therewithal
Be she likewise one of those
That an acre hath of nose
Be her teeth ill hung or set
And her grinders black as jet
Be her cheeks so shallow too
As to show her tongue wag through
Hath she thin hair, hath she none
She's to me a paragon.

—ROBERT HERRICK, "Be My Mistress Short or Tall"

Exuberance is beauty.

—WILLIAM BLAKE, *The Marriage of Heaven and Hell*

The insane, on occasion, are not without their charms.

—KURT VONNEGUT, *The Sirens of Titan*

Beauty, like truth, is relative to the time when one lives and to the individual who can grasp it.

—attributed to Gustave Courbet

I love to hear her speak, yet well I know
That music hath a far more pleasing sound:
I grant I never saw a goddess go,—
My mistress, when she walks, treads on the ground.
And yet, by heaven, I think my love as rare
As any she belied with false compare.

—William Shakespeare,
"My Mistress' Eyes Are Nothing Like the Sun"

Human feeling is like the mighty rivers that bless the earth; it does not wait for beauty—it flows with restless force and brings beauty with it.

—George Eliot, Adam Bede

Telltale Symptoms

I think table and I say chair,
I buy bread and I lose it,
whatever I learn I forget,
what this means is I love you.

—Gloria Fuertes, "I Think Table and Say Chair"

She's got most of the symptoms—is twittery and cross, doesn't eat, lies awake, and mopes in corners.

—Louisa May Alcott, *Little Women*

When a man is really in love he can't help looking like a sheep.

—AGATHA CHRISTIE, *The Mystery of the Blue Train*

I do not love thee!—yet, I know not why,
Whate'er thou dost seems still well done, to me:
And oft in my solitude I sigh
That those I do love are not more like thee!
…I know I do not love thee! yet, alas!
Others will scarcely trust my candid heart;
And oft I catch them smiling as they pass,
Because they see me gazing where thou art.

—CAROLINE ELIZABETH SARAH NORTON,
"I Do Not Love Thee"

Where there is love there is life.

—attributed to MOHANDAS KARAMCHAND GANDHI

Infatuation is one of those slightly comic illnesses which are at once so undignified and so painful that a nice-minded world does its best to ignore its existence altogether…but this boil on the neck of the spirit can hardly be forgotten either by the sufferer or anyone else in his vicinity.

—MARGERY ALLIGHAM, *The Fashion in Shrouds*

I crave your mouth, your voice, your hair,
Silent and starving, I prowl through the streets…
I want to eat your skin like a whole almond.

—PABLO NERUDA, "Sonnet XI," *100 Love Sonnets*

When you are courting a nice girl an hour seems like a second. When you sit on a red-hot cinder a second seems like an hour. That's relativity.

—attributed to ALBERT EINSTEIN

...love has made my judgment poor—
but one fact I am deadly certain of:
all the world's beauty that may cause alarm
and all of art contriving nature's charm
could never fill me with a wilder love.

—LOUISE LABÉ, "Poem XXI"

Heaven, I'm in heaven.
And my heart beats so that I can hardly speak.
And I seem to find the happiness I seek
when we're out together
dancing cheek to cheek.

—IRVING BERLIN, "Cheek to Cheek"

Quite a Compliment

Impetuous wild cow, supreme lady commanding
    the god An
Who dares not worship you?

—ENHEDUANNA,
"Inanna and the City of Ururk" (c. 2300 B.C.)

Shall I compare thee to a summer's day?
Thou art more lovely and more temperate.

—WILLIAM SHAKESPEARE, "Sonnet XVIII"

(i do not know what it is about you that closes
and opens; only something in me understands
the voice of your eyes is deeper than all roses)
nobody, not even the rain, has such small hands

—E. E. CUMMINGS,
"somewhere i have never traveled, gladly beyond"

Skin which glistens
shining over your limbs
like milk being poured
from jugs at dinnertime;
your hair is a herd of goats
moving over rolling hills...

—NUALA NI DHOMNAILL,
"Labysheedy (The Silken Bed)"

Out of all those kinds of people,
you've got a face with a view.

—DAVID BYRNE,
"Naïve Melody (This Must Be the Place)"

I don't have enough time to celebrate your hair.
One by one I should detail your hairs and
    praise them.
Other lovers want to live with particular eyes;
I only want to be your stylist.

—Pablo Neruda, "Sonnet XIV," *100 Love Sonnets*

Thou art the best of me.

—John Donne, "Song"

No simpering lips nor looks can breed
Such smiles as from your face proceed.
The sun must lend his golden beams,
Soft winds their breath, green trees their shade,
Sweet fields their flowers, clear springs their streams,
Ere such another smile be made.

—Aurelian Townsend, "To the Lady May"

The first man to compare the cheeks of a young woman to a rose was obviously a poet; the first to repeat it was possibly an idiot.

—SALVADOR DALI, as quoted in the preface of *Dialogues with Marcel Duchamp*

Why do birds suddenly appear
ev'ry time
you are near?
Just like me
they long to be
close to you.

—HAL DAVID AND BURT BACHARACH, "Close To You,"

She walks in beauty, like the night
Of cloudless climes and starry skies
And all that's best of dark and bright
Meet in her aspect and her eyes…

—LORD BYRON (a.k.a. George Gordon), "She Walks in Beauty"

Complaints

A fine romance!
With no kisses!
A fine romance,
my friend, this is!
We should be like a couple of hot tomatoes, but
    you're as cold as yesterday's mashed potatoes.

—DOROTHY FIELDS, "A Fine Romance," as sung by
    Fred Astaire and Ginger Rogers in *Swing Time*

Is it not strange that desire should so many years
outlive performance?

—WILLIAM SHAKESPEARE, *Henry IV Part II*

People who cannot make love make money.

-JAMES ARTHUR BALDWIN,
Tell Me How Long the Train's Been Gone

Went to the garden to pick a posy,
Passed the lavender, passed the lily,
Passed the pinks and roses red—
Picked a nettle sting instead.

-TRADITIONAL WELSH SONG, "Stanzas for the Harp"

Call me irresponsible,
yes, I'm unreliable,
but it's undeniably true,
I'm irresponsibly mad for you!

-FRANK SINATRA,
"Call Me Irresponsible," written by Sammy Cahn

Happiness isn't good enough for me! I demand euphoria!

—CALVIN, as written by Bill Watterson, *Calvin and Hobbes 10th Anniversary*

I personally think we developed language because of our deep need to complain.

—attributed to LILY TOMLIN

Declarations of Love

O Love, how thou art tired out with rhyme!
Thou art a tree whereon all poets climb.

—DUCHESS MARGARET CAVENDISH OF NEWCASTLE,
"Love and Poetry"

Love demands expression. It will not stay still, stay silent, be good, be modest, be seen and not heard, no. It will break out in tongues of praise, the high note that smashes the glass and spills the liquid.

—JEANETTE WINTERSON, *Written on the Body*

Her wit
so sharp
then hit
my heart

My heart
to love
her wit
doth move

Her wit
with art
doth knit
my heart

My heart
with skill
her wit
doth fill

—SIR ARTHUR GORGES, "Her Face"

It is the illusion of all lovers to think themselves unique and their words immortal.

—HAN SUYIN, *A Many-Splendored Thing*

I am two fools, I know,
For loving, and for saying so
In whining poetry.

—JOHN DONNE, "The Triple Fool"

They that are rich in words, in words discover
That they are poor in that which makes a lover.

—SIR WALTER RALEIGH, "The Silent Lover"

To try to write love is to confront the muck of language: that region of hysteria where language is both too much and too little, excessive and impoverished.

—ROLAND BARTHES, *A Lover's Discourse: Fragments*

I like not only to be loved, but to be told that I am loved. I am not sure that you are of the same mind. But the realm of silence is large enough beyond the grave. This is the world of light and speech, and I shall take leave to tell you that you are very dear.

—GEORGE ELIOT, in an 1875 letter

Did I create you in the world of fancy
Or are you my creator?
Am I the first whom inspiration blessed
Or was it you? Who writes this verse?
Did I write it for you or you for me?
…When we met first I found my beginning.

—ILYAS ABU SHABAKA, "You or I?"

Unrequited Love

I must sing of that which I would rather not,
so bitter am I toward him who is my love…
my kindness and courtesy make no impression
    on him,
nor my beauty, my virtue or my intelligence;
so I am deceived and betrayed,
as I should be if I were unattractive

      —LA COMTESSE DE DIA, "I Must Sing of That"

Nothing takes the taste out of peanut butter quite
like unrequited love.

      —CHARLES SCHULTZ AND CLARK GESNER,
        You're a Good Man, Charlie Brown

To love somebody
Who doesn't love you
Is like going to a temple
And worshiping the behind
Of a wooden statue
Of a hungry devil.

—LADY KASA, as quoted in *Women Poets of the World*

Love has nothing to do with what you are expecting to get—only with what you are expecting to give—which is everything.

—KATHERINE HEPBURN, *Me*

I'm sure you hate to hear
that I adore you, dear,
but grant me, just the same,
I'm not entirely to blame,
for you'd be so easy to love…

—COLE PORTER, "Easy to Love," from *Born To Dance*

It was the kind of desperate, headlong, adolescent calf love that he should have experienced years ago and got over.

—AGATHA CHRISTIE, *Remembered Death*

When someone asks, "Why do you think he's not calling me?" there's always one answer—"He's not interested." There's not ever any other answer.

—FRAN LEIBOWITZ, as quoted in *Mirabella*

I waited
For the phone to ring
And when at last
It didn't,
I knew it was you.

—ELEANOR BRON, "No Answer,"
The Pillow Book of Eleanor Bron

The hope I dreamed of was a dream,
Was but a dream; and now I wake,
Exceeding comfortless, and worn, and old
For a dream's sake.

—CHRISTINA ROSSETTI, "Mirage"

Beware of allowing a tactless word, a rebuttal, a rejection to obliterate the whole sky.

—attributed to ANAÏS NIN

In three words I can sum up everything I've learned about life: It goes on.

—attributed to ROBERT FROST

Sometimes with one I love, I fill myself with
rage, for fear I effuse unreturn'd love;
But now I think there is no unreturn'd love—the
pay is certain, one way or another;
(I loved a certain person ardently, and my love
was not return'd,
Yet out of that, I have written these songs).

—WALT WHITMAN,
"Sometimes with One I Love," *Leaves of Grass*

Public Opinion

Love, I find, is like singing. Everybody can do enough to satisfy themselves, though it may not impress the neighbors as being very much.

—ZORA NEALE HURSTON, *Dust Tracks on the Road*

Don't blame me, ladies, if I've loved. No sneers
if I have felt a thousand torches burn,
a thousand wounds, a thousand daggers turn
in me, if I have burnt my life with tears.
Especially, leave my good name alone.
If I have failed, my hurt is very plain.

—LOUISE LABÉ, "Sonnet XXIV"

I don't know why everything has to be so sordid
        these days…
I can take some sentiment—
tell me how charmed you were
when he wrote both your names and a heart
        in spilt coffee—
anything except that he carved them on the
        eldern tree.
But have it your way.
Picking apart your personal
dream landscape of court and castle
        and greenwood
isn't really up to me.
So call it magical. A fair country.
Anyway you were warned.

—LIZ LOCHHEAD,
"Tam Lin's Lady," *The Grimm Sisters*

The hottest places in hell are reserved for those who, in times of great moral crisis, maintain their neutrality.

—DANTE ALGHIERI, *La Divina Commedia*

They don't hardly make 'em like him any more—but just to be on the safe side, he should be castrated anyway.

—HUNTER S. THOMPSON, in an interview, 1973

He'd make a lovely corpse.

—CHARLES DICKENS, *Martin Chuzzlewit*

His mother should have thrown him away and kept the stork.

—attributed to MAE WEST

She is a water bug on the surface of life.

> —GLORIA STEINEM, in a 1992 interview

She looks like something that would eat its young.

> —attributed to DOROTHY PARKER

Her only flair is in her nostrils.

> —PAULINE KAEL,
> as quoted in *Ladies Home Journal*, 2000

If I can stop one heart from breaking,
I shall not live in vain.

> —EMILY DICKINSON, "Part One: Life"

Happy is he who causes scandal.

—attributed to SALVADOR DALI

I am the love that dare not speak its name.

—LORD ALFRED BRUCE DOUGLAS, *Two Loves*

No government has the right to tell its citizens when or whom to love. The only queer people are those who don't love anybody.

—RITA MAE BROWN,
speech at the 1982 Gay Olympics

If homosexuality is a disease, let's call in queer to work. "Hello. Can't work today, still queer."

—ROBIN TYLER,
as quoted in *The New York Times*, 1997

Love is love. Gender is merely spare parts.

—WENDY WASSERSTEIN, *The Sisters Rosenweig*

If everybody minded their own business…the world would go round a good deal faster than it does.

—LEWIS CARROLL, *Alice's Adventures in Wonderland*

Not for me the cold, calm kiss
Of a virgin's bloodless love;
Not for me the saint's white bliss,
Nor the heart of a spotless dove,
But give me the love that so freely gives
And laughs at the whole world's blame.

—ELLA WHEELER WILCOX, "I Love You"

It will not do. I must be
steaming with love, colored
like a flamingo. For what?
To have legs and a silly head
and to smell, pah! like a flamingo
that soils its own feathers behind?
Must I go home filled
with a bad poem?
And they say:
Who can answer these things
till he has tried?

—WILLIAM CARLOS WILLIAMS,
"To a Friend Concerning Several Ladies"

Completely Besotted

Morning wind in the garden
opens blossoms.
The key to my locked spirit is
your laughing mouth.

—EMPRESS NUR JAHAN (c. 1646 A.D.)

My love for you is more
Athletic than a verb.

—SYLVIA PLATH, "Verbal Calisthenics"

It has
soil
and roots
and a poppy
on top,
your mouth
a poppy.

—Pablo Neruda, "Ode to a Secret Love"

Only those who will risk going too far can possibly find out how far one can go.

—attributed to T. S. Eliot

I love you more than my own skin.

—Frida Kahlo, in a 1935 letter to Diego Rivera

My skin is alive
with the soft imprint
of your mouth.
How many miracles
can there be?
—Cynthia Fuller, "Fire Roses"

Restless, incautious, I want to talk violence,
Speak wild poems, hush, be still, pray grace
Taken forever; and after, lie long in the dense
Dark of your embrace, asleep between earth
    and space.
—Marie Ponsot, "Among Women"

For a moment when you held me fast in your
    outstretched arms
I thought the river stood still and did not flow.
—Tzu Yeh (3rd century A.D.), "Song of Tzu Yeh"

When we were first together as lover and
  beloved
We had nothing to learn; together we improved
On all the world's learning, and bettered it,
  and loved.

—VALENTINE ACKLAND,
"Teaching to Shoot," *The Nature of the Moment*

The Steamy Stuff

i like my body when it is with your
body. It is so quite a new thing.
Muscles better and nerves more.
i like your body. i like what it does.
i like its hows. I like to feel the spine
of your body and the trembling
-firm-smooth ness and which i will
again and again and again
kiss...

—E. E. CUMMINGS,
"i like my body when it is with your"

Sex between a man and a woman can be wonderful, provided you can get between the right man and the right woman.

—attributed to WOODY ALLEN

'Tis true, 'tis day; what though it be?
O wilt thou therefore rise from me?
Why should we rise, because 'tis light?
Did we lie down, because 'twas night?

—JOHN DONNE

I'll come up and make love to you at five o'clock.
If I'm late, start without me.

—attributed to TALLULAH BANKHEAD

Disrobe.
And let miracles begin.
I am speechless
before you.
Your body speaks all languages.

—Nizar Qabbani, "Poems"

I have drunk of the wine of life at last, I have
known the thing best worth knowing, I have been
warmed through and through, never to grow
quite cold again till the end.

—Edith Wharton

In this world,
love has no color—
yet how deeply
my body
is stained by yours.

—Izumi Shikibu, "In this world"

Love: I am luminous
careless as love's breathing
fluorescent glowing the fine
warm veins and bones
your weight,
the sky lowered suddenly
I am loved: a message
clanging of a bell in silence

—JOYCE CAROL OATES, "How Gentle"

to wake and find you sitting up in bed
with your black hair and gold skin
leaning against the white wall
a perfect slant of sunlight across your chest as if God
were Rembrandt or maybe Ingmar Bergman

—LESLÉA NEWMAN,
"Possibly," *Love Me Like You Mean It*

Today it rains all over the world and we are two
you and I
a man and a woman
like all the men and all the women
searching for the ark to ride out the storm.
We are two in the night and our bodies
are rays laying siege to the shadows.

      —ROSARIO MURILLO, "Angel in the Deluge"

That evening
my garden awoke
The fingers of the wind
unhinged its fences
Grasses swayed, flowers bursting,
fruits ripening
in the blissful dance of wind and rain.

      —FADWA TUQAN, "In the Flux"

Long Distance

We did many pure and beautiful things.
Now that you are leaving the city,
love's sharp pain encircles my heart.

—Sappho

O mistress mine, where are you roaming?
O stay and hear, your true love's coming,
That can sing both high and low.
Trip no further, pretty sweeting.
Journeys end in lover's meeting,
Every wise man's son doth know.

—William Shakespeare, *Twelfth Night*

Absence, that common cure of love…

—MIGUEL DE CERVANTES, *Don Quixote de la Mancha*

Judge not my passion, by want of my skill,
Many love well, though they express it ill;
And I your censure could with pleasure bear
Would you but soon return, and speak it here.

—ANNE FINCH,
Countess of Winchilsea, "A Letter to Dafnis"

To think that you and I, divided by trains and
    nations,
we had only to love one another:
with all the confusions, the men and the
    women,
the earth that makes carnations rise, and makes
    them bloom!

—PABLO NERUDA, "Sonnet II"

When my self is not with you, it is nowhere.

> —HELOISE, in a letter to Peter Abelard

We never leave each other.
When does your mouth
say goodbye to your heart?

> —MARY TALLMOUNTAIN,
> "There Is No Word for Goodbye"

Love has changed the face of distances,
we have grown closer, blending into one another.
...You are the heart's homeland, its history.

> —'ABD AL-'AZIZ AL-MAQALIH, "Nineteeth Telegram"

The Agony and the Ecstasy

Love is a fire. But whether it is going to warm your hearth or burn down your house, you can never tell.

—attributed to JOAN CRAWFORD

Love is a snowmobile racing across the tundra and then suddenly it flips over, pinning you underneath. At night, the ice weasels come.

—MATT GROENING, *Love Is Hell*

"I hate" she alter'd with an end
That follow'd it as gentle day
Doth follow night, who like a fiend
From heaven to hell is flown away:
"I hate" from hate away she threw,
and sav'd my life, saying "not you."

—WILLIAM SHAKESPEARE,
"Those Lips That Love's Own Hand Did Make"

She did observe, with some dismay, that, far from
conquering all, love lazily sidestepped practical
problems.

—JEAN STAFFORD, "The Liberation"

Love was a terrible thing. You poisoned it and
stabbed at it and knocked it down in the mud—
well down—and it got up and staggered on,
bleeding and muddy and awful.

Like—Rasputin.

—JEAN RHYS, *Quartet*

Oh! Love is frantic agony, and life one throb
   of pain;
Yet I would bear its darkest woes to dream
   that dream again.

> —JANE FRANCESCA, LADY WILDE (a.k.a. Speranza),
> "Corinne's Last Love Song"

I want to love first, and live incidentally.

> —ZELDA FITZGERALD,
> in a letter to F. Scott Fitzgerald, 1919

Love takes off masks we cannot live without and
know we cannot live within.

> —attributed to JAMES ARTHUR BALDWIN

The pleasure of possessing
Surpasses all expressing
But 'tis too short a blessing,
And love too long a pain.

> —JOHN DRYDEN, "Farewell Ungrateful Traitor"

If it is your time, love will track you down like a cruise missile. If you say, "No! I don't want it right now," that's when you'll get it for sure. Love will make a will out of no way. Love is an exploding cigar which we willingly smoke.

> —LYNDA BARRY, *Big Ideas*

Give me more love, or more disdain;
The torrid or the frozen zone
Bring equal ease unto my pain;
The temperate affords me none:
Either extreme, of love or hate,
Is sweeter than a calm estate.

> —THOMAS CAREW, "Mediocrity in Love Rejected"

Let men beware of causing women to weep; God counts their tears.

—Arabic proverb

I love you no matter what you do, but do you have to do so much of it?

—Jean Illsley Clarke, *Self-Esteem*

You've got to give a little,
take a little
and let your poor heart break a little,
that's the story of,
that's the glory of love…

—Billy Hill, "The Glory of Love"

Falling Out
of Love

Why is it we don't always recognize the moment when love begins, but we always know when it ends?

—STEVE MARTIN, *L.A. Story*

Love, for both of them, had ceased to be a journey, an adventure, and essay of hope. It had become an infection, a ritual, a drama with a last bloody act, and they could both foresee the final carnage.

—MARGARET DRABBLE, *The Middle Ground*

Stupidity got us into this mess. Why can't it get us out?

—WILL ROGERS

The word I say is not the word I mean.
You listen, speak, explain and analyze—
The air is empty where our speech has been.

—JAN MONTEFIORE, "The Mistress to Her Lover"

I never forget a face, but in your case I'll be glad to make an exception.

—attributed to GROUCHO MARX

How do you know love has gone? If you said you would be there at seven and you get there by nine, and he or she has not called the police—it's gone.

—MARLENE DIETRICH,
as quoted on ABC television, 1962

And now we are moving on
like silent ships
not knowing where we've been
or where we're going, alone
in a world of pearls
and pitiless bricks.

    —PABLO NERUDA, "Ode to a Morning in Stockholm"

A night that cuts between you and you
and you and you and you
and me: jostles us apart, a man elbowing
through a crowd. We won't
look for each other, either—
wander off, each alone, not looking
in the slow crowd...

    —DENISE LEVERTOV, "People at Night"

Some cause happiness wherever they go; others, whenever they go.

—OSCAR WILDE, *The Importance of Being Earnest*

After all, my erstwhile dear,
My no longer cherished,
Need we say it was not love,
Just because it perished?

—EDNA ST. VINCENT MILLAY, "Passer Mortuus Est"

Breathe when you breathe,
Walk where you walk.
talk when you talk,
cry when you cry,
die when you die,
let go when you let go…

—ALLEN GINSBERG

Loved and Lost

...Friends,
if you wish to survive
I would not recommend
Love

—HAROLD NORSE,
"I Would Not Recommend Love," *Hotel Nirvana*

I can't go on. I'll go on.

—SAMUEL BECKETT, *Waiting for Godot*

For love is flesh, it is a
flower flooded with blood.
Did you think it was just a
little chat across a table
a snatched hour and back home again
the way gentlemen and ladies
play at it? Either love is
A shrine
or else a scar.

—MARINA TSVETAEVA, "Poem of the End"

It isn't possible to love and to part. You will
wish that it was. You can transmute love, ignore
it, muddle it, but you can never pull it out of you.
I know by experience that the poets are right:
Love is eternal.

—E. M. FORSTER, *A Room With a View*

The truth does not change according to our ability to stomach it.

—attributed to FLANNERY O'CONNOR

What we have once enjoyed we can never lose. All that we love deeply becomes a part of us.

—HELEN KELLER, *We Bereaved*

When love is gone, there's always justice. And when justice is gone, there's always force. And when force is gone, there's always Mom.

—LAURIE ANDERSON, "O Superman (For Massenet)"

O do not love too long,
Or you will grow out of fashion
Like an old song.

—W. B. YEATS, "O Do Not Love Too Long"

Well, since my baby left me
I found a new place to dwell
Well it's down at the end of lonely street
At Heartbreak Hotel.

> —ELVIS PRESLEY, "Heartbreak Hotel" written by
> Mae Axton, Tommy Durden, Elvis Presley

'Tis not love's going that hurts my days
But that it went in little ways.

> —EDNA ST. VINCENT MILLAY, *The Harp-Weaver*

Damn you! I will not grant
your cursed soul vicarious tears or a single glance...
I swear by the miracle-working icon,
and by the fire and smoke of our nights:
I will never come back to you.

> —ANNA AKHMATOVA, "You Thought I Was That Type"

'Tis better to have loved and lost than never to have loved at all.

—ALFRED, LORD TENNYSON, *In Memoriam*

Life being what it is, one dreams of revenge.

—attributed to PAUL GAUGUIN

To love and win is the best thing. To love and lose, the next best.

—WILLIAM MAKEPEACE THACKERAY, *Pendennis*

Lessons Learned

We can only learn to love by loving.

—attributed to IRIS MURDOCH

Four be the things I am wiser to know:
Idleness, sorrow, a friend and a foe.
Four be the things I'd be better without:
Love, curiosity, friendship and doubt.

—DOROTHY PARKER, *Enough Rope*

It is impossible to love and to be wise.

—Francis Bacon, *Essays*

I think all great innovations are built on rejections.

—attributed to Louise Nevelson

It is difficult suddenly to put aside a long-standing love; it is difficult, but somehow you must do it.

—C. Valerius Catallus, *Carmina*

When I stand before thee at the day's end, thou shalt see my scars and know that I had my wounds and also my healing.

—Rabindranath Tagore

Don't look forward to the day when you stop suffering, because when it comes, you'll know you're dead.

—TENNESSEE WILLIAMS,
as quoted in *London Observer*, 1958

To love is to suffer. To avoid suffering one must not love. But then one suffers from not loving. Therefore, to love is to suffer; not to love is to suffer; to suffer is to suffer. To be happy is to love. To be happy, then, is to suffer, but suffering makes one unhappy. Therefore, to be happy one must love or love to suffer or suffer from too much happiness.

—DIANE KEATON,
in *Love and Death*, by Woody Allen

It is easier to keep half a dozen lovers guessing than to keep one lover after he has stopped guessing.

—HELEN ROWLAND, "Reflections of a Bachelor Girl"

All discarded lovers should be given a second chance, but with somebody else.

—MAE WEST

I once had a girl—
or should I say
she once had me?

—JOHN LENNON/PAUL MCCARTNEY,
"Norwegian Wood"

Time wounds all heels.

—JANE SHERWOOD ACE

Just remember, we're all in this alone.

—attributed to LILY TOMLIN

And the best and worst of this is
That neither is most to blame,
If you have forgotten my kisses
And I have forgotten your name.

—ALGERNON CHARLES SWINBURNE, "An Interlude"

They are not long,
The days of wine and roses.

—ERNEST DOWSON, "Vitae Summa Brevis
Spem Nos Vetat Incohare Longam"

A single day is enough to make us a little larger or,
another time, a little smaller.

—PAUL KLEE, in a 1908 interview

Love, with very young people, is a heartless business. We drink at that age from thirst, or to get drunk; it is only later in life that we occupy ourselves with the individuality of our wine.

—attributed to ISAK DINESEN

If grass can grow through cement, love can find you at every time in your life.

—CHER, as reported in *The Times*, 1998

Love is the shit that makes life bloom,
And you never know when you might step in it.

—MICHAEL FRANTI, "Love Is the Shit"

Love is the crocodile on the river of desire.

—BHARTRIHARI (ca. 656 AD)

There is no safe investment. To love at all is to be vulnerable. Love anything, and your heart will certainly be wrung and possibly be broken. If you want to make sure of keeping it intact, you must give your heart to no one, not even to an animal. Wrap it carefully round with hobbies and little luxuries; avoid all entanglements; lock it up safe in the casket or coffin of your selfishness. But in that casket—safe, dark, motionless, airless—it will change. It will not be broken; it will become unbreakable, impenetrable, irredeemable.

—C. S. LEWIS, *The Four Loves*

Everything we do is futile, but we must do it anyway.

—attributed to MOHANDAS K. GANDHI

A beautiful thing never gives so much pain as does failing to hear and see it.

—attributed to MICHELANGELO DI BUONAROTTI

I think that the inability to love is the central problem, because that inability masks a certain terror, and that terror is the terror of being touched. And if you can't be touched, you can't be changed. And if you can't be changed, you can't be alive.

—JAMES BALDWIN,
as quoted in *The Long Road to Freedom*

Man is an idea, and a precious small idea once he turns his back on love.

—ALBERT CAMUS, *The Plague*

Love is only an evil trick played on us to achieve the continuation of the species.

—W. SOMERSET MAUGHAM, *A Writer's Notebook*

Love is an act of endless forgiveness, a tender look which becomes a habit.

—PETER USTINOV,
as quoted in *Christian Science Monitor*

I don't think of all the misery, but of all the beauty that remains.

—ANNE FRANK, *The Diary of Anne Frank*

If this is the best of all possible worlds, what are the others like?

—FRANCOIS-MARIE AROUET VOLTAIRE, *Candide*

The world breaks everyone, and afterward, some are strong at the broken places.

—ERNEST HEMINGWAY, *A Farewell to Arms*

my spirit with its loss
knows this;
though small against the black,
small against the formless rocks,
hell must break before I am lost

—H.D. (HILDA DOOLITTLE), "Eurydice"

That love is all there is
Is all we know of love.

—EMILY DICKINSON, as quoted in *The Single Hound*

The heart is forever inexperienced.

—attributed to HENRY DAVID THOREAU

Happiness

Happiness is the china shop; love is the bull.

—attributed to H. L. MENCKEN

If you were happy every day of your life you wouldn't be a human being ... you'd be a game show host.

—WINONA RYDER in Heathers,
written by Daniel Waters

Haply I think on thee,—and then of my state,
Like to the lark at the break of day arising
From sullen earth, sings hymns at heaven's gate;
For thy sweet love remembered such wealth brings
That then I scorn to change my state with kings.

—WILLIAM SHAKESPEARE, "Sonnet 29"

One grows accustomed to being praised, or being blamed, or being advised, but it is unusual to be understood.

—E. M. FORSTER, A Passage to India

When two people achieve lasting happiness, this is not solely because they are great lovers but because they are also—I must put it crudely—good people; controlled, loyal, fairminded, mutually adaptable people.

—C. S. LEWIS, That Hideous Strength

For one human being to love another: the work for which all other work is but preparation.

> —RANIER MARIA RILKE, 1904,
> in *Letters to a Young Poet*

Love is all you need.

> —JOHN LENNON/PAUL MCCARTNEY,
> "All You Need Is Love"

What the world really needs is more love and less paperwork.

> —attributed to PEARL BAILEY

Love is not enough. It must be the foundation, the cornerstone—but not the complete structure. It is much too pliable, too yielding.

> —BETTE DAVIS, *The Lonely Life*

Happiness always looks small while you hold it in your hands, but let it go, and you learn at once how big and precious it is.

—MAXIM GORKY, *The Zykovs*

Happiness is like a butterfly which, when pursued, is always beyond our grasp, but, if you will sit down quietly, may alight upon you.

—attributed to NATHANIEL HAWTHORNE

Your joy is your sorrow unmasked.
And the selfsame well from which your laughter rises was oftentimes filled with your tears.

—KAHLIL GIBRAN, "On Joy and Sorrow," *The Prophet*

Lasting Love

Little darling
I feel the ice is slowly melting
little darling
it seems like years since it's been clear
here comes the sun
here comes the sun
and I say:
It's alright…

—GEORGE HARRISON, "Here Comes the Sun"

Old doubts have vanished with old dying love.
Now joy wells up in my beloved's eyes
distilling hope and fragrance in my heart.
How distant now is that anxiety!

—Ilyas Abu Shabaka, "This Is My Wine"

You came. And you did well to come.
I longed for you and you brought fire
to my heart, which burns high for you.
Welcome, darling, be blessed three times
for all the hours of our separation.

—Sappho, "Andromache's Wedding"

Those rugged rivers of water and of threat,
torturous pavilions of the foam,
incendiary hives and reefs: today
they are this respite, your blood in mine,
this path, starry and blue as the night,
this never-ending simple tenderness.

—Pablo Neruda, "Sonnet LIII"

Doubt the stars are fire;
Doubt the sun doth move;
Doubt truth to be a liar;
But never doubt I love.

—WILLIAM SHAKESPEARE, *Hamlet*

In time the Rockies may tumble
Gibraltar may crumble—
they're only made of clay.
But our love is here to stay.

—GEORGE AND IRA GERSHWIN,
    "Our Love Is Here to Stay"

The memories of long love gather like drifting snow, poignant as the mandarin ducks who float side by side in sleep.

—MURASAKI SHIKIBU, *The Tale of Genii*

She is coming, my own, my sweet;
Were it ever so airy a tread,
My heart would hear her and beat,
Were it earth in an earthy bed;
My dust would hear her and beat,
Had I lain for a century dead;
Would start and tremble under her feet,
And blossom in purple and red.

—ALFRED, LORD TENNYSON, "Maud"

O ancient brightness! O far off light!
Naked light, love, shine on us always.
And when the day comes when we are no more
    than stones,
After we too, my love, are only ruins,
Let us lie like these stones singing in the sun,
Leading others to love along our vanished ways.

—RAFAEL ALBERTI,
"Homecoming of Love Amongst Illustrious Ruins"

Love is the wild card of existence.

—RITA MAE BROWN, *In Her Day*, 1976.

If all would lead their lives in love like me,
Then bloody swords and armour should not be;
No drum nor trumpet peaceful sleeps should
    move,
Unless alarm came from the camp of love.

—THOMAS CAMPION, "My Sweetest Lesbia"

It requires infinitely greater genius to make love
than to make war.

—NIN DE LENCLOS,
The Memoirs of Ninon de L'Enclos

In the ease of love
the wretch feels himself a man,
builds up faith in life…

> —Pier Paolo Pasolini,
> "Sex, Consolation for Misery"

What does love look like? It has the hands to help others. It has the feet to hasten to the poor and needy. It has eyes to see misery and want. It has the ears to hear the sighs and sorrows of men. That is what love looks like.

> —St. Augustine, *Confessions & Enchiridion*

I believe that unarmed truth and unconditional love will have the final word in reality.

> —Rev. Dr. Martin Luther King, Jr.,
> Nobel Prize acceptance speech, 1964